LIVING IN
ASIA

Living in INDIA

Jen Green

W
FRANKLIN WATTS
LONDON·SYDNEY

Franklin Watts
First published in Great Britain in 2016 by The Watts Publishing Group

Credits
Series Editor: Julia Bird
Series Design: D.R. ink

ISBN 978 1 4451 4862 5

Picture credits: AJP/Shutterstock: 6t, 11t. V.S. Anandhakrishna/Shutterstock: 4t, 18t. Banana Republic Images/Shutterstock: front cover, 18b. Shishir Bansai/Dreamstime: 14t. Youssouf Cader/Dreamstime: 8b. cornfield/Shutterstock: 10b. Dennis Cox/Alamy: 21t. Crepesoles/Shutterstock: 15t. crshelare/Shutterstock: 7t. Natalia Davidovich/Shutterstock: 12b. costas anton dumitresco/Shutterstock: 13b. Eye Ubiquitous/Alamy: 15b. Andrey Gudkov/Shutterstock: 19b. javaman/ Shutterstock: 13t. Arnab & Manisha Maity/Shutterstock: 20b. Alexander Mazurkevich/Shutterstock: 14b, 19t. Neil McAllister/Alamy: 17. Mikadun/Shutterstock: 8c. monotoomono/Shutterstock: 6b. Ami Parikh/Shutterstock: 8t, 20t. Saikat Paul/Shutterstock: 5b. David Pearson/Alamy: 9t. Pikoso.kz/Shutterstock: 5t. paul prescott/Shutterstock: 12t. daniel prudek/ Shutterstock: 13c. Radio Kafka/Shutterstock: 9b, 22b. rkifoto/Shutterstock: 16t. Helene Rogers/Alamy: 11b. Anubhab Roy/ Shutterstock: 16b. sunsetman/Shutterstock: 7b. szefei/Shutterstock: 20c. tanrtrik71/Shutterstock: 21b. Dana Ward/ Shutterstock: 16c. Zigroup Creations/Shutterstock: 10t.

Printed in Malaysia

Franklin Watts
An imprint of
Hachette Children's Group
Part of The Watts Publishing Group
Carmelite House
50 Victoria Embankment
London EC4Y 0DZ

An Hachette UK Company
www.hachette.co.uk

www.franklinwatts.co.uk

Contents

Words in bold are in the glossary on page 23.

Welcome to India

Hello! I live in India.

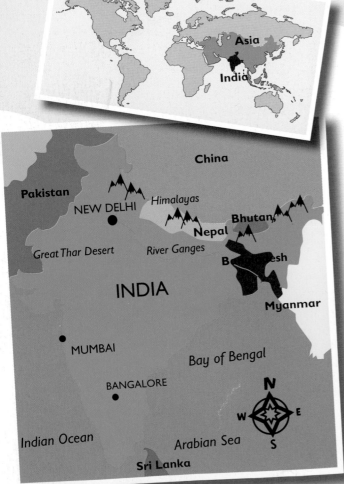

Where is India?

India is a large country in southern Asia. It is the world's seventh largest country. It shares **borders** with China, Pakistan, Bangladesh, Nepal, Bhutan and Myanmar. There are high mountains on the northern border. India has a long coastline, washed by the Indian Ocean and the Arabian Sea.

Regions of India

India has many different **landscapes**. There are snowy mountains, sandy deserts, wide **plains** and thick forests. Each part of India has its own language and **customs**, and people even wear different clothes.

A beach in Goa, western India

What's the weather?

India has three main seasons: cool, hot and wet. Winter lasts from October to February, with snow in the mountains. Summers are hot and dry. Between June and September, winds blow in off the Indian Ocean, bringing very heavy **monsoon** rains.

Heavy monsoon rains often cause flooding

People in India

I was born in India. My country has many people. One sixth of all the people in the world come from India.

Where people live

India has 1.2 billion people. China is the only country with more people. Two-thirds of people live in the countryside, but India's cities are growing fast. India is a very **ancient** country. Over the centuries, many peoples have settled in India, including Muslims from Central Asia.

A crowded street in Mumbai

Languages

People speak different languages in different parts of India. The main language is Hindi, but each region has its own language. In school, children learn their lessons in Hindi and English, but may speak a different language at home.

Religion

Religion is very important in India. Most people are Hindus. The Hindu religion has many gods and goddesses. Many other Indians are Muslims, and there are also Sikhs, Christians and Buddhists.

Hindu temples have many statues of gods and goddesses.

Cities

India has many cities. I come from New Delhi, the Indian **capital.** *It has two parts: the ancient town of Delhi, and the modern capital, New Delhi.*

Government buildings in New Delhi

India has over forty cities with more than one million people.

Biggest city

India's cities are growing fast as people move from the countryside to find work. Mumbai, a busy **port** on the west coast, is the very biggest city. It has many factories, which produce cars, trucks, steel and computers.

Modern industries

The city of Bangalore in southern India has many high-tech industries. Companies here make computer **software**. People also work in **call centres**, answering telephone calls for international companies, such as banks.

Getting around

Indian cities are very crowded during rush hour when people travel to and from work. City streets are clogged with cars, trucks, buses, scooters, cycles and small taxis called tuk-tuks. It gets very noisy as drivers toot their horns!

A busy street in the city of Kolkata

Country life

Most Indians live in villages in the countryside. My family lives in a small village in central India.

Work

Most country people work as farmers. Each family has a small plot of land where we grow our food. The main crops grown in India are rice, tea, sugar cane, wheat, **millet** and lentils. Some country people are skilled at pottery, wood-carving, embroidery and metal work.

When the villagers of Kanha grow enough crops, they sell them at market.

A team of oxen plough a field.

Way of life

Few Indian farms have tractors. Instead, we use **oxen** to pull ploughs and carts. Many villages don't have electricity or a supply of fresh water. We use oil lamps and draw water from the well.

Collecting water from a well.

Family

Families are very important in India. Grandparents, parents and children often live in one house. When a girl marries, she usually goes to live with her husband's family.

Landscape and wildlife

India is a huge country with many different kinds of scenery. We live in a dry, sandy **desert** in northwest India. Other parts of India are very wet, with lush forests.

The Himalayas

Mountains and plains

The snowy Himalayas form the northern border of India. These are the world's highest mountains. South of the mountains is a huge, flattish plain, watered by rivers such as the Ganges. This area is good for growing crops.

Southern India

Southern India forms a huge triangle of land jutting out into the ocean. This area is mostly a high **plateau** edged by hills covered with forests. There are beautiful beaches on the coast.

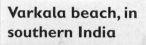

Varkala beach, in southern India

Yak

Wildlife

Each part of India has different animals. Snow leopards, bears and shaggy cattle called yaks live in the mountains. Camels carry people across deserts. Tigers, rhinos, deer, peacocks and elephants live deep in the forests.

Camels in the Thar Desert

What we eat

In India we like our food hot and spicy! We also like it sweet. I love eating gulab jamun!

Gulab jamun, an Indian sweet

North and south

Each part of India has its own style of cooking. The most popular dishes are spiced vegetables, served with a thick lentil soup called dhal. In northern India this is eaten with flat bread called chapattis or with naan bread. In southern India we eat dhal with rice.

Naan bread

Meat or vegetables?

In India what we eat partly depends on our religion. Muslims don't eat pork. Hindus don't eat beef, and many don't eat meat at all, only tasty beans and vegetables. The most popular meat dish is **tandoori** chicken. It is cooked in a clay oven.

Samosas are a favourite snack. These little pastries are filled with spicy potatoes, onions and peas.

Customs

Often people eat sitting cross-legged on the floor. We use our fingers or bread to scoop up the food. Food may be served in little metal dishes. In southern India we often use banana leaves as plates!

People eat their meal off banana leaf plates.

Having fun

There are lots of things to do in India. People have fun playing sport and board games and going to films.

In polo, teams on horseback hit the ball with long sticks called mallets, and try to score a goal.

Sports

India's favourite sport is cricket. It's played on the streets, in open grassy spaces and on the beach. Hockey, football, badminton and polo (see left) are also popular.

Boys playing cricket

Board games and kabaddi

We like to play cards and board games. Chess and snakes and ladders were both invented in India long ago. If you want to be more active, try kabaddi! This team game is like a cross between tag and wrestling.

Bollywood

Indians are mad about films. India's own film industry is based in Mumbai. It's called Bollywood. India produces over 800 films a year – more than Hollywood in the USA.

Bollywood film posters

Famous places

India has hundreds of amazing places to visit. People come from all over the world to see the sights.

Made of marble

The Taj Mahal is India's most famous building. It was built by a Muslim **emperor** in memory of his wife, and is made of white marble. Muslim emperors called the Mughals ruled India for almost two hundred years.

Holy places

People go on journeys called **pilgrimages** to visit holy places. The Golden Temple of Amritsar is a holy site for Sikhs. The Ganges is a holy river for Hindus. People visit the city of Varanasi to pray and bathe in the Ganges.

People bathing in the Ganges at Varanasi

Tiger reserves

Bandhavgarh Tiger **Reserve** is a great place to see tigers. Tigers are now rare because hunters kill them for their beautiful skins.

Seventy per cent of the world's tigers live in India.

Festivals and holidays

*India is famous for its **festivals**. There are Hindu, Muslim, Sikh and Christian festivals and other holidays, so there's always something going on!*

Hindu festivals

Diwali is a Hindu New Year festival. People give presents and light candles. The spring festival of Holi is great fun. People throw coloured water and powder paint over each other.

Lighting candles at Diwali

Having fun at Holi

Honouring the cow

The southern festival of Pongal honours cows, which are decorated with flowers. Hindus believe that cows are holy. Across India, they are allowed to wander freely through the streets. Sometimes they cause traffic jams because no one shoos them away!

Statue of Mahatma Gandhi (1869–1948)

Celebrating independence

The British ruled India in the 1800s, but Indians wanted to be independent. A great leader called Mahatma Gandhi led the struggle for **independence**. In 1950 India became an independent **republic**. Republic Day is celebrated with fireworks and parades.

India: Fast facts

Capital: New Dehli

Population: 1.2 billion (2013)

Area: 3,287 million sq km

Official languages: Hindi, English and 21 other official languages

Currency: Indian rupee

Main religions: Hinduism, Islam, Christianity, Sikhism, Buddhism, Jainism

Longest rivers: Brahmaputra, 2,850 km; Ganges 2,525 km

Highest mountain: Kangchenjunga, 8,586 m

National holidays: Republic Day (26 January), Independence Day (15 August), Mahatma Gandhi's birthday (2 October), Diwali and Holi (Hindus), Eid ul-Fitr (Muslims), Vaisakhi (13 or 14 April, Sikh New Year), Easter, Christmas Day (25 December, Christians)

Glossary

ancient very old

border a line marking the boundary between two countries

call centre an office where workers answer phone calls for businesses

capital city where the country's government meets

customs a traditional way of doing things, that has been followed for many years

desert a large area of very dry land

emperor the ruler of an empire, a territory which is made up of several countries

festival a celebration, usually for religious reasons

independence when a country gains freedom from control by another country

landscape the natural scenery

millet a cereal crop that is used to make flour

monsoon a wind that brings heavy rain at certain times of year

oxen plural of ox, a strong animal in the cow family

pilgrimage a religious journey

plain a large area of flat land

plateau an area of flat land on high ground

port a town by the sea which provides a good harbour for ships

republic a country that is ruled by leaders elected by the people

reserve a protected area for wildlife

software programs and operating systems used by computers

tandoori a way of cooking meat in a clay or metal oven

Index